THE HARD WORK OF HEALING

THE HARD WORK OF HEALING

Edited by **Brandon Gimbel**, M.D.

Michael Blumberg, L.C.P.C. | **Carl Jerome**
Tory Krone, A.M., L.C.S.W. | **Reverend Katie Snipes Lancaster**
Alan J. Levy, Ph.D. | **Rabbi Steven Stark Lowenstein**
Tovah Means, M.S., L.M.F.T. | **Nancy Perlson**, L.C.S.W., R.Y.T.
Jason Price, L.M.F.T. | **Jean Schwab**, M.S.W., L.C.S.W. | **Courtney Wells**, Ph.D.

NORTH STAR
BEHAVIORAL HEALTH

The Hard Work of Healing
© 2025 North Star Behavioral Health

Printed in the United States of America. All rights reserved. No part of this book may be reproduced or transmitted in any form or by any means, electronic or mechanical, including photocopying, recording, or by any information storage and retrieval system, without written permission from the publisher.

The information in this book is provided for informational purposes only. The authors are not rendering medical advice. Neither the editor nor contributors assume any liability for loss, damage, or disruption caused by errors or omissions, whether such errors or omissions result from negligence, accident, or any other cause. Some names and identifying details have been changed to protect privacy.

NO AI TRAINING: Without limiting the exclusive rights of the authors and publisher under copyright, any use of this publication to "train" generative artificial intelligence (AI) technologies is expressly prohibited. The publisher reserves all rights to license uses of this work for AI training and development of machine learning language models.

ISBN (paperback): 979-8-9999485-0-2
ISBN (ebook): 979-8-9999485-1-9

Edited by Brandon Gimbel, M.D.
Associate Editor Jill Bailin Rembar
Design Marko Markovic, 5mediadesign

Published by North Star Behavioral Health
www.northstarbh.com

CONTENTS

Note on Patient Stories 7
About the Contributors 9
About the Editor 13

Introduction:
The Hard Work of Healing 15

Brandon Gimbel, M.D.
Staying With What Hurts 19

Michael Blumberg, L.C.P.C.
The Limits of Control 25

Tory Krone, A.M., L.C.S.W.
It's Okay to Take Up Space:
A Journey Toward Self-Acceptance 29

Jason Price, L.M.F.T.
Staying Present Through Betrayal 35

Courtney Wells, Ph.D.
"I'm Broken": Trauma and the Fear
of Being Too Much 39

Tovah Means, M.S., L.M.F.T.
Finding Safety to See What Was Hidden 43

Nancy Perlson, L.C.S.W., R.Y.T.
Healing in the Liminal Spaces 47

Carl Jerome
Letting Go of the Story: Returning to Raw Data 51

Alan J. Levy, Ph.D.
Living Relationships 57

Reverend Katie Snipes Lancaster
The Embodied Shape of Grief 61

Rabbi Steven Stark Lowenstein
Carrying the Wound Together 65

Jean Schwab, M.S.W., L.C.S.W.
Living With What Cannot Be Fixed 69

Afterword 75
Acknowledgments 77

NOTE ON PATIENT STORIES

The clinical stories in this book are composites. All names, identifying details, and timelines have been changed to protect privacy. These vignettes are solely for educational and reflective purposes and should not be interpreted as referring to any actual patient or case.

ABOUT THE CONTRIBUTORS

Michael Blumberg, L.C.P.C., is the founder and director of Glenview Counseling Group, where he specializes in treating OCD and related disorders. He completed post-graduate training with the IOCDF's Behavioral Therapy Training Institute and has presented locally, nationally and internationally on OCD and ERP. He is a former board member of OCD Midwest and a founding member of the Chicagoland Hoarding Task Force.

Carl Jerome is the founder of North Shore Meditation and Dharma Center and DeepDharma.org, where he teaches mindfulness and meditation, as well as Buddhist philosophy and psychology. In addition, the Center offers instruction in mindfulness psychology for those seeking to relieve their anxiety, stress, depression, trauma, and other mental health challenges.

Tory Krone, A.M., L.C.S.W., is the founder and clinical director of Proactive Therapy, a group practice in Chicago that has been serving clients for over a decade. She specializes in eating disorders as well as evidence-based approaches, including Acceptance and Commitment Therapy (ACT) and the Gottman Method of couples therapy. She is especially interested in helping people foster deeper, more meaningful connections—with themselves and others.

Reverend Katie Snipes Lancaster is a Presbyterian (U.S.A.) pastor. She finds time to write in the string of silence just before dawn.

Alan J. Levy, Ph.D., is a psychoanalyst practicing in Northfield, Illinois. He trained at the National Institute for the Psychotherapies in New York and has held faculty positions at Columbia University, USC, Loyola, and the University of Chicago. His work focuses on relational psychoanalysis and helping adults navigate life's complexities through deep, ongoing therapeutic engagement.

Rabbi Steven Stark Lowenstein is currently the Senior Rabbi at Am Shalom Congregation in Glencoe, Illinois. Since his ordination by Hebrew Union College in Cincinnati, he has served as a rabbi in Chicago for the past thirty years with a focus on pastoral care and human relationships.

Tovah Means, M.S., L.M.F.T., is an owner, psychotherapist, and teacher at Watch Hill Therapy in downtown Chicago. Her work focuses on treating complex and extreme relational trauma, and she is especially interested in helping people reconnect with their authentic selves after trauma.

Nancy Perlson, L.C.S.W., R.Y.T., is a trauma-informed therapist in private practice in Illinois and Utah. Her work focuses on grief, traumatic loss, and life transitions, using somatic and integrative approaches to support healing.

Jason Price, L.M.F.T., is a licensed marriage and family therapist and co-owner of Affiliates in Counseling, a group psychotherapy practice serving the Chicagoland area. His clinical work centers on helping clients understand how they seek to get their emotional needs met through relationships, while exploring the origins of their thoughts, behaviors, and patterns. Jason works with individuals, couples, and families, and also specializes in supporting high-achieving athletes across collegiate and professional sports.

Jean Schwab, M.S.W., L.C.S.W., is a therapist operating her own private practice. Her work includes a variety of therapeutic approaches and focuses on individuals facing life-threatening illnesses and coping with grief and loss.

Courtney Wells, Ph.D., is a clinical psychologist and founder of Pivot Psychological Services, where they support individuals and couples working through trauma and reconnecting with themselves and each other. They also teach part-time at the University of Chicago and DePaul University, where they get to nerd out about psychology, systems, and the power of collective healing. Courtney has a special love for working with Queer folx and brings a deep commitment to Queer studies, liberation, and cultivating spaces for expansion.

ABOUT THE EDITOR

Brandon Gimbel, M.D., is a board-certified psychiatrist and psychotherapist. He is the founder of North Star Behavioral Health, a private practice group in the Chicago area focused on thoughtful, relationship-centered care. As editor of *The Hard Work of Healing*, he brought together voices from across the healing professions to explore what real care looks like in practice. Dr. Gimbel teaches psychiatry residents at Rush University Medical Center and writes about the human side of psychiatric work. His clinical approach emphasizes humility, clarity, and the slow, complex process of real healing.

INTRODUCTION: THE HARD WORK OF HEALING

BRANDON GIMBEL, M.D.

This book began with a simple idea: to bring together exceptional voices from across the healing professions. I sought out therapists, clergy, and mindfulness teachers, and I asked them to write honestly about what healing actually looks like—not in theory or in branding language, but in real life. In rooms, in relationships, in the quiet, private places where change begins.

I wasn't in search of clean narratives or polished essays. I asked for small, reflective pieces, each grounded in lived experience. Some of the contributors gathered here are colleagues I know well, while others I've admired from afar. Together, these writers have created something textured, uneven in the best ways, and deeply human.

These offerings are not sweeping or definitive claims about what healing is. They are glimpses, from different angles, into what healing can be—how it feels, how it moves, and how, often, it is not about fixing but about staying present, staying connected, and staying in the work.

Many of the reflections that follow circle this same truth, but in different forms, through different lenses. Together, they offer a shared invitation: to look closely, to stay longer, and to trust that healing often begins right here.

I hope you find something in these pages that resonates, shifts your understanding, and leaves you seeing something familiar in a new way.

1.

STAYING WITH WHAT HURTS

BRANDON GIMBEL, M.D.

I once worked with a parent—let's say a father, successful and driven—who came to therapy, ostensibly, not because of anything wrong in his own life, but because his child was struggling. In this case, we'll say it was his daughter.

This isn't the story of one parent or one child. It's a composite, drawn from a pattern I've seen many times, as parents begin to mourn the child they'd imagined, and try to accept the one who is in front of them, who is different from the child their imagination had created.

This fellow's daughter was anxious and sensitive, struggling to find her place in a world that didn't seem built for her. Her father was consumed by it—by her sensitivity, by her difference, by what it seemed to say about her, and what it seemed to reflect about him. He focused on her failures, on the glaring mismatch between his accomplishments and hers, and he worried about how it looked to his friends, to his coworkers, and maybe even to his family. No one said anything directly, but he imagined their judgments anyway.

And then he adjusted. He hid who his daughter really was, or lied about her, to preserve a version of himself he could still be proud of. Underneath it all was fear: fear that his child would never "get it together," never fulfill the life he had imagined for her, or for himself through her. That fear turned to frustration, and that frustration turned to anger—sharp, cutting outbursts that left them both ashamed.

He came to therapy armed with strategies: books he'd read, goals he'd set, theories he was eager to try. He was ready to fix something. But it became clear he couldn't fix his daughter. That wasn't the work. The work was facing the grief and fear of loving her as she was, not who he hoped she would be. It meant mourning the version of her he had imagined, and the version of himself that depended on that image.

He began to see that the stories he told weren't about her at all; they were about him—his disappointments, his unmet expectations, the painful mismatch between the child he imagined and the person in front of him. Slowly and painfully, he saw that he had been causing his child pain, not because of who she was but because he kept rejecting her for not being someone else.

It wasn't a sudden epiphany, but a gradual shift. And relative to the years of denial and wishful thinking, of trying to will a different version of her into being, those few months of therapy felt to him like they went fast.

He began to accept her—not perfectly, but more than before. And she did better. The anger lifted, mostly his, some of hers, and they grew closer.

But then came the harder part: accepting who he had been. He had to sit with the years he had treated his child harshly and face the fact that his responses had been more about his pain than hers. He saw that guilt could not undo damage; it could only name it. His task now was not erasure but showing up differently, knowing what he had already missed.

For any parent this is incredibly hard: to face not only a child's pain but one's own role in it. Many never do. Some distance themselves, rationalize, or shut the door once the crisis has passed. But he stayed.

And something else grew—not erasure or forgetting, but a new kind of closeness, grounded in honesty, tenderness, and the ongoing work of acceptance.

The pain that brought him to therapy did not disappear, but it changed. It loosened. It no longer ruled him. Not because his child changed, but because he did.

I start with this story because it captures something central to healing—not just in my work, but in the reflections that follow. Time and again, we see that healing begins not with fixing but with staying.

People don't come to therapy to optimize themselves or build resilience. They come because they're in pain. Because of grief, fear, regret—the sense that something is broken. Or already lost.

In most of medicine, pain is a signal. Patients feel it, seek help, and act. In psychiatry, pain is harder to see. It is psychic, emotional, existential—and easier to rationalize or minimize. Healing begins when we can simply say, *something is wrong*. From there, we try to understand the source of the pain. Sometimes that leads to change. More often, the work is not about solving the pain but about learning to stay with it.

Mindfulness helps us see. It means noticing, on purpose, what the mind does. And what most people notice, when they look closely, is that their thoughts think themselves. Minds don't wait to be asked. They problem-solve, rehearse, ruminate, and loop back to the same painful ideas over and over.

But mindfulness is not only attention. It includes self-compassion—the ability to notice suffering without judgment, to witness it with curiosity instead of critique. That small shift changes everything, and I have found it to be useful for my patients—and for myself.

Acceptance is the harder work. Not approval, not surrender. Just saying: *this is here, this hurts, and I am willing to feel it.*

That shift, from resisting to allowing, is where healing begins. It does not feel like a breakthrough. It feels like sitting with something we have avoided for years—grief, regret, helplessness—and not flinching.

That is what the father did. Not only by understanding, but by staying. And maybe that is the point: we only begin to understand once we stay.

Mindfulness helps us see. Acceptance helps us stay. And staying, again and again, becomes the work.

Not to be better. But to be here, fully, with what is.

2.

THE LIMITS OF CONTROL

MICHAEL BLUMBERG, L.C.P.C.

Truth be told, while I do care about you, I don't much care about your feelings. Childhood milestones are irrelevant to me and I am breathlessly bored by your relationships. Don't tell me about your mother's drinking or your father's affairs. And whatever you do, and this cannot be overstated, do not tell me your dreams. Tell me only your thoughts and describe your behaviors and do exactly as I tell you and you will begin to feel better.

If ever there was a caricature of a cognitive behavioral therapist, this would be it. And for a time, I lived that caricature. It was my creed, too.

Cognitive behavioral therapy, better known as CBT, is an effective treatment for many psychological disorders and presentations. For the sake of brevity, it can be summed up by three basic suppositions and a theory to link them together. It supposes that (a) we cannot choose our feelings, (b) we cannot control which thoughts occur to us, but we can change them once they enter our awareness, and (c) we have full control of our behaviors. Therefore, if we change our maladaptive behaviors and challenge our distorted thinking we will begin to feel better.

The effectiveness of CBT is, in many cases, truly staggering. Studies have shown that for certain conditions—like OCD,[*] panic disorder, and specific phobias—it can lead to significant symptom reduction in more than 80 percent of patients.

---

[*] Obsessive-compulsive disorder.

That said, CBT does not offer 100 percent efficacy in the treatment of any one condition. Which is to say: not everyone who is treated with CBT gets better.

I recall an incident at an OCD case consultation group that I used to run with a colleague. We were discussing a complicated case in which the clinician had tried virtually all CBT interventions to no avail. I interjected, saying that perhaps another modality of therapy was indicated. For just a moment my colleagues glared at me as though I had suggested that we adopt the geocentric model of planetary movement. But the moment quickly passed, and we began to have a hearty discussion of other potential interventions to help the patient.

In my experience, most therapists fall into one of two blind spots—depending on their training. Those who practice traditional psychotherapeutic modalities such as psychoanalysis or Rogerian therapy are guilty of the first of these: They do not use evidence-based treatments (EBTs) such as CBT—even when those would be the most effective place to start. On the other hand, those of us who are staunch practitioners of EBTs can fall into the oppositive trap, as illustrated in my example above: We tend to keep using the same tools, even when they are clearly not working.

People are greater than the sum of their symptoms. Treating symptoms alone, without considering the complexity of the human condition, may hamper efforts to achieve the best possible outcomes. As I grow older I find that my firmly held beliefs about therapy and, indeed, the world at large, are beginning to soften. I am working to trade dogma for nuance. I believe it's for the best.

3.

IT'S OKAY TO TAKE UP SPACE: A JOURNEY TOWARD SELF-ACCEPTANCE

TORY KRONE, A.M., L.C.S.W.

These are the symptoms Lara checked off on her intake form: increased appetite, trouble concentrating, difficulty sleeping, low self-esteem, depressed mood, anxiety, hopelessness, nightmares.

She arrives in my office all smiles and jokes—as if she's supposed to entertain me. She doesn't seem like someone who struggles socially. Do her friends know she feels hopeless? I wonder.

She says she's here to work on anxiety.

Months into therapy, she casually mentions she goes to Weight Watchers every Saturday, where people clap if the number on the scale goes down. If her weight goes up—even slightly—she feels ashamed. She logs every bite of food. The number of points at the end of the day tells her how to feel about herself.

It's in my office that she first hears the words: eating disorder. Just because others are also obsessed with food and bodies—and seem to manage well enough—doesn't mean that life is workable for her.

One week, she tells me she went out to dinner with friends. I ask her to write down the thoughts she'd had during the meal—to go back and capture what was running through her mind.

She returns with a page full of scribbles:

Don't touch the bread. You won't stop.

You already ate too much today.
The dressing will go straight to your thighs.
After she reads it aloud, I ask, "So how was the dinner conversation?"

She pauses. She doesn't remember it.

I have her close her eyes and imagine the same dinner, but without focusing on food or her body. "If you weren't caught up in those thoughts, what would you want to make the night about?"

She smiles. "I'd have asked more questions and listened to the answers. Connected with my friends. Talked about things that matter."

That's where healing begins—not with the absence of pain, but with noticing what the pain has crowded out.

A year later, Lara has thrown her scale away. Stopped counting calories. She tells me she feels a freedom she's never experienced before.

But healing isn't linear.

One day she comes in upset—she weighed herself after yoga and now feels guilt and shame. I sense anger too—not just at herself, but maybe at me. Therapy gave her freedom, but it took away control.

We retrace what led to that moment. Her mother, who can be anxious and demanding, was visiting.

"Her visit was overwhelming. I was so annoyed with her, but I feel bad. She didn't really do anything wrong." Then she pauses. "She was just being herself."

I offer: "Sounds like being around your mom made you feel the same way that stepping on the scale does—overwhelmed, angry, guilty."

She nods.

We talk about how food and control became ways to manage emotions that she didn't feel she was allowed to express. When she shares childhood memories, she never criticizes her family—only herself. "I always felt like I was too much. Too loud. Too emotional. Too opinionated."

I couldn't imagine her without these traits that seemed essential to her being. A loud laugh. An unfiltered opinion. An exaggerated hand gesture with a curse word. I'd laugh along, hoping she'd notice—that maybe those parts weren't too much. Maybe they were just right.

Years later, she's planning her wedding. She tells me she's not trying to fit into a dress—instead, she's finding one that fits her. But stress still sneaks in. Some sessions, she spirals about how she'll look.

I don't reassure her. I have her close her eyes. "Picture it," I say.

Together, we build the scene: the vows, the dancing, the people who love her. Later, she writes it all down—to revisit when her mind tries to convince her she needs to be different.

She's learning that healing isn't about fixing herself. It's the ability to slow down and ask:

What do I need in this moment?

What is this feeling really about?

If I stopped struggling, what would I move toward?

What do I want to organize my life around?

Her healing occurs when the pressure to shrink returns, but instead of retreating into control, she closes her eyes and remembers the altar, her partner, the music, the joy. She doesn't calculate or self-correct.

She reminds herself:

It's okay to take up space.

4.

STAYING PRESENT THROUGH BETRAYAL

JASON PRICE, L.M.F.T.

I retrieve a couple from my waiting room. The wife walks briskly ahead, while the husband lags behind. They enter my office and sit on the couch opposite my chair. Almost immediately, the husband hunches forward, elbows on his knees, eyes fixed on the floor. His wife turns sharply toward him, her posture tense.

I offer some small talk to ease us in, but she cuts me off.

"You just don't get it," she says to her husband. "You have no idea how much you continue to hurt me."

This is our fifth session. They came to therapy after it was discovered that the husband had been gambling, putting them in financial jeopardy. They are raw and hurting. He feels ashamed for the secret gambling behavior that got them here. She feels betrayed and exhausted—forced into the role of being the responsible one in their marriage.

This scene is common in couples therapy: one partner feeling hurt and betrayed, the other drowning in guilt and shame. Healing often begins here—in the discomfort and the pain.

Couples enter therapy uncertain whether their relationship can survive. But even in the aftermath of betrayal, there's an opportunity—not just to repair the relationship, but to heal parts of the self that have been hurting since childhood.

We're drawn to partners for more than shared interests or because of chemistry. A deeper longing lies beneath: to be seen, soothed, and loved in ways we may have missed in our families of origin. These unmet needs often surface in moments of crisis.

Couples therapy helps couples heal by accessing those underlying emotions and childhood wounds. The wife's anger masked more vulnerable fears: *Can I trust you? Will you take care of me?* She grew up in a divorced home with an absent father and a mother who worked long hours. Her anger was a desperate attempt to shake her husband out of emotional withdrawal, to push him to be stronger and more present for her . . . but in reality, it pushed him further away. His silence wasn't indifference, it was protection. He had grown up with undiagnosed ADHD,* struggled in school, and was harshly punished by his parents. He internalized the belief that he wasn't good enough, and learned to retreat inward to avoid criticism.

Couples therapy gave them the space to see each other differently. The wife learned to express her pain without blaming. The husband learned to stay emotionally present without collapsing into shame. As she shared her childhood abandonment and her desire for a "real partner," he began to empathize. As he opened up about his feelings of failure and powerlessness, she softened. His betrayal began to make sense—not as something done to her, but as an enactment of a long-standing self-fulfilling prophecy.

---

* Attention-deficit/hyperactivity disorder.

Healing happened as they offered each other what they had never received. He truly heard her in a way her parents never did. She responded by nurturing the part of him that had always felt inadequate. He took tangible steps to rebuild trust—joining a recovery group, opening up financially, taking accountability. She praised his efforts, affirmed his strength, and became a voice of support.

Over time, their sessions held moments of quiet connection. The wife cried, and instead of turning away, the husband reached out and held her hand. He didn't try to fix it—he was simply present for her.

Healing in couples therapy is about creating something new—a more honest and emotionally attuned relationship. For this couple, the crisis that brought them to therapy became an opening for a deeper connection and an opportunity to heal wounded parts of themselves.

5.

"I'M BROKEN": TRAUMA AND THE FEAR OF BEING TOO MUCH

COURTNEY WELLS, PH.D.

Trauma can have a profound impact on a person's fundamental sense of self. "I'm broken" is a belief that can emerge, quietly at first, before amplifying until it's pervasive, for folx* who have experienced trauma. Even when logical assessment says otherwise, in a felt sense, they experience themselves as deficient or lacking, as incapable of finding or keeping love, as incompetent and incapable of creating the life they want or feel they previously had. Broken in the aftermath of trauma.

For some people, trauma is a disruption. You are going along in life and startlingly, trauma happens, disrupting your trajectory. The desire to "return" to life as it was before is often profound—how could it not be? Well-meaning friends and family can echo this hope in their effort to support their loved one "getting back to who you are." Often, when we want to "get back to" something, what we are really saying is "forget what happened." But forgetting is the illusion. Healing requires remembering—and staying with what changed.

For some people, trauma is a fact of life—something they have known from the start. There is no "before" to which they can return. Rather, what exists is a deep desire

---

* Folx is an intentional spelling variation of "folks," used to signal inclusion of LGBTQ+ and other marginalized identities. In this chapter, the term is used in the spirit of that inclusivity.

to escape, to create a life different from what they have known. Despite this longing, they often feel trapped by the very survival strategies that worked so well for them in the past. But these strategies—guarding, numbing, avoiding—often become barriers to the life they want.

Relationships can be profoundly impacted when folx have experienced trauma. Survival learning, especially when trauma has occurred in the context of a relationship, tells us that relationships aren't worth it. It whispers, *Relationships are where trauma happens, they should be avoided,* or, at the very least, entered into with caution. The probability of feeling misunderstood in relationships is strong; fears may not be understood, the desire to protect yourself and others may be misinterpreted, and the effort it takes to *not* react can go unnoticed. Even when one yearns for intimacy, intimacy can be incredibly threatening, an impossible bind that can be confusing for you and others.

While we are not able to forget terrible traumatic events, or unlearn old strategies of survival—an incredibly frustrating reality of human cognition—we are built to learn. Even if early learning taught us that vulnerability is perilous or that anxiety means there's danger here, we can learn to *do* these moments differently. We can learn to *do* vulnerability, even when fear is present.

Healing is hard; even the word creates the illusion of an end point. But like growing, there is no finish line. No final destination. Rather, healing is an ongoing process—a commitment to learning new ways of responding to trauma-prompted emotions and patterns. That commitment is required because of how wildly hard the work is. It seems simple when concisely identified in a reflection on healing, and while it may be simple, it is anything but easy. Taking small, measured risks of vulnerability in relationships, even trusted ones, can feel like walking on a tightrope suspended over a canyon.

When I reflect on healing and trauma, I am struck by the immense amount of courage it asks of folx to feel the fear and take the step anyway. Physical healing can sometimes be thought of as passive; you break a bone, wear a cast: healed. But healing after trauma is an active rebuilding in the face of intense emotions. It's like trying to build a house in the midst of a storm, laying each brick with a quiet hope and fierce determination—not to outlast the storm, but to live beyond it.

6.
FINDING SAFETY TO SEE WHAT WAS HIDDEN

TOVAH MEANS, M.S., L.M.F.T.

What do you do if you feel pain but can't find the source? When your bones cry out for healing, but your eyes can't locate the injury? Some pain is easy to identify and treat, while other kinds are invisible—unconscious, felt in the body but with roots the mind can't fully recognize. And without being able to see the injury, how can you apply medications, treat the wound, or set the bones right, allowing them to finally heal and scar over? Such "invisible" injuries have the power to cripple us.

As a child, I was aware of vague emotional pains that only grew louder as I aged, but they didn't present themselves in ways I knew how to address. There was no clear source, there were no visible injuries. My suffering was invisible—even to myself. What eventually clued me in to my own distress signals was a desperate longing for healing. Though I remained trapped for quite some time, unable to access information about my wounds, my orientation toward healing carried me across the country—from the East Coast to the Third Coast—where I became a therapist. More importantly, it's where others got to know me well enough to help me uncover the invisible origins of my suffering.

In graduate school, I began to understand trauma not just as a dramatic event, but as a wound—especially one that shapes the mind's development in the context of threat or disconnection. I began to understand that our minds behave differently when they feel unsafe, especially with someone close to us whom we depend on. When danger—real or perceived—feels overwhelming, our minds may dissociate from the experience entirely. And in cases of chronic childhood trauma, that dissociation can become so frequent, so embedded, that the person no longer sees the trauma for what it was. It becomes invisible—even to the one who lived through it.

As I learned about trauma, I traced my own experiences. *Did I go through this?* The answers weren't in my mind, but in my body—which buzzed in nonverbal agreement. The word *trauma* eventually unlocked ancient doors of defense, allowing me to finally locate my injuries. At the same time, sitting with other trauma survivors as a therapist showed me that I wasn't alone. Many people feel real pain yet struggle to find its source.

I've come to understand that some injuries are hidden away for our own protection—especially those that occurred in childhood at the hands of the very people we depended on. Ultimately, you can't heal what you can't acknowledge. And often, you can't acknowledge what would have made surviving childhood feel impossible. We go blind to protect ourselves, and we only regain sight when it finally feels safe enough to see again. I was first wounded in the arms of those who were supposed to love me. But in the arms of others—kind, steady, caring—I began to come back to life.

The epitome of healing—for myself and the trauma survivors I work with—has been finding physical and emotional safety in order to see and heal the wounds of childhood trauma.

7.
HEALING IN THE LIMINAL SPACES

NANCY PERLSON, L.C.S.W., R.Y.T.

Following is a brief list of vivid images that came to mind as I reflected on the many forms healing has taken over the years in my practice as a clinical social worker:

    An unexpected laugh
    Holding a hard truth
    Saying "I'm sorry"
    Discovering a unique definition of forgiveness that finally feels right
    Going to the grocery store you've been avoiding
    Responding to a text or email—or making an actual phone call
    Listening to messages
    Deleting messages
    Awe at a sunset... or really, any experience in nature that takes your breath away
    Running into someone you didn't expect to see, and crying... or not crying
    Walking up or down the stairs unassisted
    Going back to work
    Quitting your job
    Cooking a favorite meal
    Showering
    Discovering you're a painter
    Saying "no"... or "yes"
    A moment of unmitigated joy

There's a theme here, right? Well, no—not exactly. And that, I suppose, is the point.

Healing is deeply personal. But it's often misunderstood. We carry a quiet cultural assumption that healing is a destination—something to achieve or complete. That idea spreads easily, absorbed without question. But it's false.

And we know it in the deepest place of our beings.

We are always healing, just as we are always growing, changing, and evolving. I know healing when I see it. It's a feeling—a moment of significance. A spark. And if we pause to notice, giving that spark the attention it deserves, we may feel the weight of it—the gravity of what's shifting—and sometimes, the relief that comes with it.

Healing is not something to be perfected or completed; there's no linear, set pattern to follow. Rather, it exists in the liminal spaces between then and now and what's to come. It begins in subtle shifts, again and again—often unplanned—where we begin to see ourselves and the world through a new lens. These moments may seem small, but they matter. And if we stay with them, they can carry us into something new—the beginning of a different way of being.

The moments I describe as "healing" are born of time, patience, and a willingness to hold the unknown in a vulnerable surrender. Not the kind that feels like giving up —but a surrender that feels like release. A softening. A quiet trust that something else might emerge.

In our pain and despair, we must dare to believe that something different is possible—and hope that this "something" might be better than what we are currently experiencing.

At our core is the muscle of resilience that, as it strengthens, opens the path to healing. Hope feeds that muscle. Healing, in turn, ignites imagination, self-compassion, and curiosity—essential elements on the path toward a new kind of wholeness. A wholeness that embraces, embodies, and invites not just joy, but our pain and brokenness, simultaneously—the very things that move us to explore the outermost edges of what it means to be human.

8.
LETTING GO OF THE STORY: RETURNING TO RAW DATA

CARL JEROME

My background in Buddhist psychology has taught me that emotions don't arise from people, places, things, or events themselves. Rather, they are internal responses—primitive reflexes shaped by our nervous systems. This idea has long been held in Buddhist tradition—for over 2,700 years—sometimes explained through the concept of the *Five Aggregates*, and more recently supported by scientists like Dr. Lisa Feldman Barrett, author of *How Emotions Are Made*.

There is considerable evidence that emotions, developed as adaptive mechanisms for survival, can also be maladaptive. In other words, the amygdala, the part of the brain that quickly sorts safe from unsafe and affinity from aversion, often gets it wrong. Thus, we can end up reacting to situations with fear, shame, or anger that isn't fully warranted—believing those emotions as truth. When this happens, we can get stuck. But that stuckness isn't permanent. It can be healed.

Consciousness is our awareness that our mind creates narratives directing our actions under particular circumstances. As Barrett explains, these narratives come from memories, understandings of emotion from experiences, and the present situation.

A narrative—our self-talk and self-defining story— emerges from raw sensory input. We see, hear, touch, smell, taste, and think. In Buddhism, thinking is considered a sixth sense, because it plays as central a role in shaping experience as any other. The mind takes in this sensory data and, based on the amygdala's split-second appraisal of safe vs. unsafe, pleasant vs. unpleasant, it adds a positive or negative charge. These emotions become embedded in the narratives we tell ourselves. Over time, these stories can harden into identity.

This is one way to understand the first of the Five Aggregates in Buddhism: form (our body and senses) as the foundation upon which perceptions and feelings give rise to internal narratives. Contemporary science echoes this: As Dr. Barrett describes, emotions are not fixed reactions—they're constructed interpretations layered onto experience.

Healing occurs nonetheless, even when we firmly believe our painful narratives. How is that possible? Our minds present these narratives as truth. We identify with them. We appropriate them as "who we are." If we didn't believe our narratives, we would be paralyzed and unable to choose, which is not what evolution developed us to do.

The answer lies in considering narratives as useful stories, rather than static truths, and then examining them at the level of "raw data." Here's an example:

Narrative: "It's too hot to jog, and tomorrow it will rain. I hate this weather because it never lets me prepare for the marathon."

Raw data: The temperature is 89 degrees.

The narrative, unconnected to what is happening, triggers emotions like resentment and anger. But the raw data suggests possibilities such as a shorter run outside, use of an indoor track, or cross-training, all helpful for the upcoming marathon.

Shirley (not her actual name, though the rest is true) came to me terrified she was going to die of cancer and not live to play with her new "grandbabies." She told me she didn't believe in traditional medicine and was going to a German clinic for treatments that have not been approved in this country.

I shared an analogy with Shirley that I hoped would lessen her narrative and its attendant emotions while allowing her to treat the cancer as she felt appropriate, to heal her psychic pain and suffering. I focused on the raw data, saying: "When your nails get chipped, you go for a pedicure. When your hair gets too long, you go to the salon. When you have cancer, you go to the doctor for treatment."

The raw data does not contain a narrative about dying, grandbabies, treatment as failure, or justified anger; instead, it suggests a less painful path. Go to a cancer specialist and follow a treatment plan. It's just like going to a nail salon for a pedicure, or a beautician for a styling. It is mindfulness on steroids, awareness without a narrative—a healthy, healing, beneficial attitude. For the next nine years, Shirley received infusions and other treatments at the German clinic to boost her immune system.

We saw each other weekly as she let the analogy settle in, then monthly, and currently we talk occasionally online. Shirley has only three tumors now and is being treated by a specialized oncologist who practices Western medicine. The doctor is optimistic, and so is Shirley. I am, too.

The raw data without a painful narrative can be healing. I've seen this approach ease the long-term effects of trauma in many forms: a woman in her sixties who had survived systematic abuse as a child; a recent college graduate still carrying the weight of severe bullying during high school; and an adult patient confronting the echoes of early relational rupture.

It has been ten years since I first met Shirley. She continues her treatments, and between them, she flies around the country to play with her grandchildren.

9.

LIVING RELATIONSHIPS

ALAN J. LEVY, PH.D.

When I was a young child, I had the opportunity to be in psychoanalytic treatment. This was very unusual for a boy who grew up in a lower middle-class blue-collar neighborhood in the Bronx. I took the subway down to Manhattan by myself to meet with my analyst in what appeared to me to be a sophisticated office worthy of James Bond. I remember heading home on the subway deep in thought, while thinking about nothing and everything at once. My memories of my treatment were not so much of the insights that I gained about my life and my family per se. What I now know is that I was in a very different state of mind, a sort of trance state that reached deeply into unconscious ways of thinking and understanding. I remember the importance of my relationship with my analyst, his understanding and empathy, and his acts of kindness. He became a pillar in my life that has stayed with me to this day. I remain convinced that psychoanalytic treatment saved me from living a very difficult life. My relationship with him set me on a life course that led me to becoming a psychoanalyst myself.

As a psychoanalyst, I try to embody this sense of healing, of deep empathy and understanding, genuinely feeling with and caring about my patients. To me, empathy and understanding are created in relationships between people and not given. I also have learned in my psychoanalytic training that empathically feeling with patients is not always possible. It is especially important during these times to listen for a lack of connectedness or rupture and to recognize that these too are valuable forms of communication. Though the relational road may be rocky, I learned the importance of not being too quick to think that I know, and to give my patients and myself the chance to find each other, especially when that is daunting. This connection allows something new to emerge, where my patients can negotiate their lives and feel alive in them.

Perhaps most important, I have come to understand that the vicissitudes of my relationships with my patients are themselves primary vehicles for growth. I have learned that true analytic healing lies in the ongoing attempt to understand our experience and not simply in the understanding itself. Indeed, understanding oneself and others, though essential, follows from experiencing within meaningful relationships. To me, healing is a verb, not a noun.

While all forms of healing strive to reduce human suffering, I believe that psychoanalytic treatment, along with allied forms of therapy, aims to help people live more fully and deeply. I find that the unfolding, living relationships that I develop with my patients, throughout their difficulties and their triumphs, are opportunities for the process of understanding what has been injurious to them and their hopes and dreads. As I have learned, analytic treatment is a mutual but an asymmetrical process. It is only through relationships that I can engage patients in a process that engenders exploration, understanding, and growth for their benefit.

After all, in the end, all I have is myself, my experience, my knowledge, and my passion to heal.

10.

THE EMBODIED SHAPE OF GRIEF

REVEREND KATIE SNIPES LANCASTER

"**G**rief is hard, actually the hardest of emotions... it requires a willingness to bear the unbearable." Serene Jones knows grief. First, she lost a pregnancy, then her marriage collapsed, and a dear friend died. In the next moment, illness, both sudden and chronic, found its way into her body, and soon, half a dozen other life-altering events arrived at her doorstep. Grief came on like a storm in her body: muscles aching, temples throbbing, bone-tired, running on fumes, mind wandering. Amid all this, she did what she had always done—teach theology, but all the while, losing her faith. Places where she had once thrived, from the spiritual to the academic, faded. The streams ran dry. It wasn't until she acknowledged a deep and deepening body-grief connection that a door opened. Her own body—heartbeat and breath, flesh and bone—became for her an entryway into healing, letting her live amid the raw, tender incompleteness that feels fresh and new in a world of loss. "Healing, if it comes, happens in the midst of things."

As a pastor, I witness this same embodiment: grief is tangible and bone-deep. Even when that slip-through-your-fingers texture of sorrow leans in the direction of the ineffable, grief is tactile. It is beyond words and yet bodily; never disconnected from the *terra firma*, the physical. Poet Joy Katz, mourning her mother, said "Sorrow is work, and it does not satisfy." There is no map for grief, no clear mile markers or triumphant conclusion. The body knows. Grief is palpable, yet so is the possibility of healing.

The body's response to grief is not separate from how we understand our place in the world. Even our vocabulary for being human reflects this grounding. In Latin, the root word *human* comes from the word *humus*, meaning ground. In Hebrew, the root word for *human* comes from *adama*, meaning ground, earth, soil. Contemplative priest Richard Rohr puts it this way: "Being human means acknowledging that we are made from the earth and will return to the earth." This, of course, brings us to the place of death, loss, and even burial, evoking those ancient words spoken in the Christian tradition at one's graveside: "Ashes to ashes, dust to dust, earth to earth." There is a physicality to grief, and thus a physicality to the dream of healing amid such sorrow.

I am reminded of a piece of music by James Taylor—"Fire and Rain." His friend Suzie died, and his "walk through the valley of the shadow of death" was literal: one foot in front of the other, a somatic response—body first, moving, drifting, wandering. In his song, he remembers that his first instinct is to go, to walk, to get on his feet, to take to the road. His second instinct is to write a song. He couldn't sit still with his grief. Similarly, poet Wendell Berry takes a walk when the weight of despair is heavy. He says, "I go and lie down where the wood drake rests in his beauty on the water, and the great heron feeds." Our bodies carry grief out into the wild world of wonder, beauty, and sorrow, allowing us to encounter the visceral possibility of healing. May it always be this way: that we might trust the embodied nature of grief, held close by our own earthy bodies toward healing.

11.

CARRYING THE WOUND TOGETHER

RABBI STEVEN STARK LOWENSTEIN

Healing remains one of the great mysteries of our daily lives. Jewish tradition has long recognized that there are two distinct components: the healing of the body and the healing of the spirit. Medicine may no longer have the insightful monopoly on the nature of healing. True healing of the body, no matter what, must also include healing of the spirit. Healing requires uncovering a hidden integrity, a recognition that what we needed was already within us. It's about growth and our ability to get in touch with that divine spark that is deep within us. As Rabbi Nancy Flam writes: "To heal the spirit involves creating a pathway to sensing wholeness, depth, mystery, purpose and peace."

At each and every prayer service we also offer the *Mi Shebeirach* prayer. The *Mi Shebeirach* is not just for those who are sick—it is a prayer for all of us. This prayer allows quiet time for reflection and can be a moment of calming relaxation. This prayer allows us to reach our innermost thoughts and helps us get in touch with our own strength and faith. The *Mi Shebeirach* prayer itself should elevate us to a place beyond our pain and discord. It is there that we can regroup, regenerate, rekindle the divine light as it were, and return to the task of rebuilding the fragments of the world that we encounter.

My teacher and friend Debbie Friedman who wrote this most famous prayer once wrote: "In these moments of reflection, we are forced to face whatever obstacles are in the way of our living fully. While we know full well that healing of the body may not be a possibility, we know that healing of the soul has infinite possibilities." That's why we pray for both.

> *Mi shebeirach avoteinu*
> *M'kor habrachah l'imoteinu*
> May the source of strength,
> Who blessed the ones before us,
> Help us find the courage to make our lives a blessing,
> And let us say, Amen.

> *Mi shebeirach imoteinu*
> *M'kor habrachah l'avoteinu*
> Bless those in need of healing with *r'fuah sh'leimah*,
> The renewal of body, the renewal of spirit,
> And let us say, Amen.

12.
LIVING WITH WHAT CANNOT BE FIXED

JEAN SCHWAB, M.S.W., L.C.S.W.

My first experience in a healing profession was as a social work student intern with the pediatric spinal cord injury population at Shriners Hospital. Throughout that year I was mentored by many generous medical professionals and ad hoc healers, ranging from surgeons to secretaries, as I watched children and teens acclimate to life-altering spinal cord injuries. I also learned about the complications and challenges of living in a body that can no longer move, that cannot regulate its temperature, is unable to sense bowel and bladder urgency, and which can be felled by the seemingly smallest foe, a pressure ulcer.

For someone with a spinal cord injury who cannot shift their own position or sense moisture, even a small irritation on the skin's surface can be the start of a serious wound. If unaddressed, this tender spot can deepen, breaking down the layers beneath the skin, sometimes all the way to the bone. What begins as a subtle vulnerability can become a dangerous and distressing injury. This is one of the primary ways that I've come to understand healing: simply put, healing begins with awareness. Awareness that there is a problem, a breakdown, an area that needs to be examined and tended to before deeper damage takes hold.

My second professional healing role was as a pediatric oncology social worker at Lurie Children's Hospital in

Chicago, a job I held for sixteen years. During that remarkably intense, heartbreaking, and fulfilling time I developed a second understanding: that healing is a process of both holding on and letting go—a lesson forged while helping children move through cancer treatment.

Many children seem to live with an instinctive ability to stay in the present, and to accept that some things must be surrendered on the road to healing. Alex, an eight-year-old with osteosarcoma, was anxious and afraid of the surgery that would amputate his leg, yet curious and eager to be fitted for his titanium blade prosthetic. His vision of healing included playing soccer again, walking with his grandfather, and returning to outdoor recess. He was willing to part with his leg in order to hold on to the promise of mobility and activity.

Across the room, his parents grieved the serious diagnosis, the extreme treatment plan, and the uncertainty of their son's future. They could only see loss—the hardship ahead and the precariousness of his health. Alex was ready to let go. His parents were desperate to hold on. And yet, they moved forward together.

Now, as a therapist in private practice that focuses on grief and illness, my third and likely final healing role, I have come to another dimension of understanding: that healing is less often about eliminating suffering, and more often about learning how to live within its presence. It is in this stage of my work that I have come to embrace the quiet wisdom of the Japanese concept, *mono no aware*.

Mono no aware, often translated as "the pathos of things," reflects the capacity to hold both the fleeting beauty of life and the sorrow embedded in its impermanence. This sensibility allows me to sit with clients who are navigating not only illness and death, but also the profound uncertainty of simply living. Whether it is a parent facing a child's terminal diagnosis, an adult grieving the sudden loss of a spouse, or an individual confronting their own mortality, the healing process asks both client and therapist to enter into a vulnerable, honest relationship with impermanence itself.

In this therapeutic space, healing begins with awareness—just as it did with the spinal cord patients I once cared for when the first signs of sensation returned to their skin. Awareness of pain, fear, shame, or despair. But healing also requires what I witnessed with Alex: the ability to hold both grief and hope simultaneously. To let go of what can no longer be controlled, while holding on to what remains meaningful and possible.

The therapeutic relationship becomes a container for this paradox. Each session carries the fragile beauty of being both finite and profound. We are never guaranteed another hour together, yet within each hour, something essential unfolds. Clients speak what was previously unspeakable. They allow themselves to feel what they had feared might undo them. And as they do, healing emerges, not as the absence of pain, but as an expanded capacity to live honestly in its presence.

Mono no aware reminds me daily that healing is not a clean, resolved end point, but a living process that honors both the tenderness of what is lost and the resilience of what remains. As therapists, we do not erase suffering. We walk with our clients into the depths of their humanity, trusting that within this honest, vulnerable, and time-bound relationship, something deeply healing takes root.

AFTERWORD

BRANDON GIMBEL, M.D.

From outside the worlds of psychotherapy, ministry, or mindfulness, these practices may look nearly identical: people sitting together, talking, listening, creating space for vulnerability. Inside each tradition, of course, the divisions are sharp. Some prize symptom reduction, others, insight and meaning. Yet I have long believed that the best practitioners, wherever they begin, often arrive in the same place.

Self-awareness. Acceptance. Compassion. Patience.

That is what this collection demonstrates. Across different disciplines, these voices return to the same ground. Healing does not belong to one profession. It emerges in the shared humility of facing human experience together.

I have learned from my colleagues here. And I will continue to learn—from them, and from my constant teachers: my patients.

ACKNOWLEDGMENTS

BRANDON GIMBEL, M.D.

My thanks to the contributors to *The Hard Work of Healing* for the thoughtfulness and care they brought to their writing. Each chapter reflects their depth of experience and commitment to their work.

I am also grateful to Jill Bailin Rembar, whose steady hand helped shape this collection into its final form.

Finally, my thanks to my colleagues at North Star Behavioral Health; to my fellow clinicians, for always prioritizing our patients; and to Susan Shade, for the invisible daily work that keeps us all afloat.

Brandon Gimbel, M.D.

www.ingramcontent.com/pod-product-compliance
Lightning Source LLC
LaVergne TN
LVHW041345080426
835512LV00006B/623